C

Knock-Knock Jokes for Kids

Find Charlie the Cavalier on Facebook, Instagram, Pinterest, and Twitter.

CharlieTheCavalier.com

The Charlie the Cavalier Puppet can be used to tell the jokes in this book. Find the Puppet for free at CharlieTheCavalier.com.

Copyright © 2015

No part of this book can be reproduced without permission from the author.

Knock, knock!
Who's there?
Doris.
Doris who?
Doris locked that's why I am knocking!

Knock, knock!
Who's there?
Ken.
Ken who?
Ken I come in, it's freezing out here?

Knock, knock!
Who's there?
Howl.
Howl who?
Howl you know unless you open the door!

Knock, knock!
Who's there?
Carrie.
Carrie who?
Carrie on with what you're doing, I'm at the wrong door!

Knock, knock!
Who's there?
Cow goes.
Cow goes who?
No, cow goes "Moo!"

Knock, knock!
Who's there?
Ketchup.
Ketchup who?
Catch up with me and I'll tell you!

Knock, knock!
Who's there?
Boo.
Boo who?
Please don't cry. It is only a joke!

Knock, knock!
Who's there?
Tank.
Tank who?
You're welcome!

Knock, knock!
Who's there?
Lettuce.
Lettuce who?
Lettuce in!

Knock, knock!
Who's there?
Noah.
Noah who?
Noah good place to eat?

Knock, knock!
Who's there?
Who.
Who who?
You never told me you're an owl!

Knock, knock!
Who's there?
Olive.
Olive who?
Olive you.

Knock, knock!
Who's there?
Europe.
Europe who?
Europe early today!

Knock, knock!
Who's there?
Cargo.
Cargo who?
Car-go beep, beep!

Knock, knock!
Who's there?
Dwayne.
Dwayne who?
The bath tub is Dwayne-ing.

Knock, knock!
Who's There?
Dewey.
Dewey who?
Dewey have to go home?

Knock, knock!
Who's there?
Justin.
Justin who?
Justin time for lunch.

Knock, knock!
Who's There?
Barbie.
Barbie Who?
Barbie Q Chicken!

Knock, knock!
Who's there?
Kiwi.
Kiwi who?
Kiwi go to the store?

Knock, knock!
Who's there?
Ice cream.
Ice cream who?
Ice cream if you don't let me in!

Knock, knock!
Who's there?
Police.
Police who?
Police may I come in?

Knock, knock!
Who's there?
Water.
Water who?
Water you doing in my house?

Knock, knock!
Who's there?
Tank.
Tank who?
You're welcome!

Knock, knock!
Who's there?
Nobel.
Nobel who?
No bell, that's why I knocked!

Knock, knock!
Who's There?
Theodore.
Theodore who?
Theodore is locked!

Knock, knock!
Who's there?
Mikey.
Mikey who?
Mikey is lost please let me in!

Knock, knock!
Who's there?
Stopwatch.
Stopwatch who?
Stopwatch you are doing right now and open the door!

Knock, knock!
Who's there?
Frank.
Frank who?
Frank you for being my friend!

Knock, knock!
Who's there?
Wooden shoe!
Wooden shoe who?
Wooden shoe give me a hug?

Knock, knock!
Who's there?
Hairy.
Hairy who?
Hairy up and let us in!

Knock, knock!
Who's there?
Ivana.
Ivana who?
Ivana come in!

Knock, knock!
Who's there?
Woo.
Woo who?
Don't get too excited, it's just a joke!

Knock, knock!
Who's there?
Sherwood.
Sherwood who?
Sherwood like to come in!

Knock, knock!
Who's there?
Cash.
Cash who?
I would love to have a cashew!

Knock, knock!
Who's There?
Handsome.
Handsome Who?
Handsome food to me please!

Knock, knock!
Who's There?
Doughnut.
Doughnut Who?
Doughnut ask me!

Knock, knock!
Who's There?
Wayne.
Wayne Who?
Wayne drops keep falling on my head!

Knock, knock!
Who's there?
Owls say.
Owls say who?
Yep.!

Knock, knock!
Who's there?
Eileen.
Eileen who?
Eileene'd on the door and broke it!

Knock, knock!
Who's there?
Dewey.
Dewey who?
Dewey have to keep saying these jokes!

Knock, knock!
Who's there?
Al.
Al who?
Al give you a hug if you open the door!

Knock, knock!
Who's there!
Abbey.
Abbey who?
Let me in, Abbey just stung me!

Knock, knock!
Who's there!
Atlas.
Atlas who?
Atlas I get to spend time with you.

Knock, knock!
Who's there!
Atch.
Atch who?
I'm sorry I didn't know you were sick!

Knock, knock!
Who's there?
Police.
Police who?
Pol-e-s-e open the door!

Knock, knock!
Who's there?
A little boy.
A little boy who?
A little boy who can't reach the doorbell!

Knock, knock!
Who's there?
Pooch.
Pooch who?
Pooch your arms around me!

Knock, knock!
Who's there?
Peas.
Peas who?
Peas be my friend!

Knock, knock!
Who's there?
Yeah.
Yeah who?
Easy there cowboy!

Knock, knock!
Who's there?
Ben.
Ben who?
Ben knocking for 10 minutes!

Knock, knock!
Who's there?
Will.
Will who?
Will you open the door already?

Knock, knock!
Who's there?
Two knee.
Two knee who?
Two-knee fish!

Knock, knock!
Who's there?
Pete.
Pete who?
Pete-za delivery guy!

Knock, knock!
Who's there?
Oink oink.
Oink oink who?
Make up your mind, are you a pig or an owl!

Knock, knock!
Who's there?
Shelby.
Shelby who?
Shelby comin' round the mountain when she comes!

Knock, knock!
Who's there?
Claire.
Claire who?
Claire the way, I'm coming through!

Knock, knock!
Who's there?
Ivor.
Ivor who?
Ivor you let me in or I`ll climb through the window!

Knock, knock!
Who's there?
Rita.
Rita who?
Rita book!

Knock, knock!
Who's there?
Howl.
Howl who?
Howl you know unless you open the door?

Knock, knock!
Who's there?
Howie.
Howie who?
I'm fine, how are you?

Knock, knock!
Who's there?
Myth.
Myth who?
Myth you too!

Knock, knock!
Who's there?
Eyesore.
Eyesore who?
Eyesore do like you!

Knock, knock!
Who's there?
Lena.
Lena who?
Lena little closer and I'll tell you!

Knock, knock!
Who's there?
Pasture.
Pasture who?
Pasture bedtime isn't it?

Knock, knock!
Who's there?
Eddie.
Eddie who?
Eddie body home?

Knock, knock!
Who's there?
Jester.
Jester who?
Jester minute. I'm trying to find my keys!

Knock, knock!
Who's there?
Heaven.
Heaven who?
Heaven seen you for ages!

Knock, knock!
Who's there?
Eva.
Eva who?
Eva you are having trouble hearing or your doorbell isn't working!

Knock, knock!
Who's there?
Iguana.
Iguana who?
Iguana give you a high-five.

Knock, knock!
Who's there?
Scold.
Scold who?
Scold out here, let me in!

Knock, knock!
Who's there?
Sid.
Sid who?
Sid down and have a drink!

Knock, knock!
Who's there?
Luck.
Luck who?
Luck through the peep hole and you'll find out!

Knock, knock!
Who's there?
Repeat.
Repeat who?
Who Who!

Knock, knock!
Who's there?
Warrior.
Warrior who?
Warrior you have been all my life?

Knock, knock!
Who's there?
Isaiah.
Isaiah who?
Isaiah nothing till you open this door!

Knock, knock!
Who's there?
Honey bee.
Honey bee who?
Honey bee a dear and open the door!

Knock, knock!
Who's there?
Herd.
Herd who?
Herd you were home, so I came right over!

Knock, knock!
Who's there?
Shirley.
Shirley who?
Shirley you must know me by now!

Please look for other **Charlie the Cavalier books**, the Charlie the Cavalier Busy book, and Charlie the Cavalier Jokes books on Amazon.

Made in the USA
Monee, IL
26 February 2023

28728202R00020